LUCI SWINDOLL

CELEBRATING LIFE!

CATCHING THE THIEVES THAT STEAL YOUR JOY

NAVPRESS

A MINISTRY OF THE NAVIGATORS
P.O. BOX 35001, COLORADO SPRINGS, COLORADO 80935

The Navigators is an international Christian organization. Jesus Christ gave His followers the Great Commission to go and make disciples (Matthew 28:19). The aim of The Navigators is to help fulfill that commission by multiplying laborers for Christ in every nation.

NavPress is the publishing ministry of The Navigators. NavPress publications are tools to help Christians grow. Although publications alone cannot make disciples or change lives, they can help believers learn biblical discipleship, and apply what they learn to their lives and ministries.

ISBN 08910-95470

Printed in the United States of America

11 12 13 14 15 16 17 / 99 98 97 96 95

FOR A FREE CATALOG OF
NAVPRESS BOOKS & BIBLE STUDIES,
CALL 1-800-366-7788 (USA)
or 1-416-499-4615 (CANADA)

CONTENTS

*Lovingly dedicated to Beth and Jeff Meberg,
whom I have watched grow up as we've
celebrated sixteen years of birthdays,
accomplishments, Thanksgivings,
Christmases, reunions, and graduations.
With this book, I now celebrate their
adulthood.*

AUTHOR

Luci Swindoll is Vice President of Public Relations for her brother Chuck's international radio ministry, *Insight for Living*. She is also a popular conference and retreat speaker who is frequently asked to speak on the topic of living and loving life.

Celebrating Life! Catching the Thieves that Steal Your Joy is Luci's seventh book. *Wide My World, Narrow My Bed* was published in 1982, followed by *The Alchemy of the Heart, You Bring the Confetti, My Favorite Verse,* and *After You've Dressed for Success.* She is also the author of a working journal entitled, *Quite Honestly,* and the editor of *Soloing: Experiencing God's Best as a Single Woman.*

Luci earned her bachelor's degree in commercial art from Mary-Hardin Baylor College in Texas and enjoyed a thirty-year career with Mobil Oil Corporation. Before choosing early retirement to join the staff of *Insight for Living* in 1987, she was an executive with Mobil's West Coast Pipelines Division in Torrance, California.

Among Luci's many interests are travel, reading, art, and music. She sang professionally for fifteen years with the Dallas Opera.

Luci lives in Fullerton, California, with her cat, Ms Ree. "That's such an appropriate name for my cat," says Luci. "Ms Ree loves company!"

ACKNOWLEDGMENT

I would like to express sincere thanks to my dear friend, Traci Mullins, the editor of this book. Traci is the best in her field. I confess honestly, were it not for her hard work and expertise, this discussion guide would not be in print.

PREFACE

Celebrating Life! Catching the Thieves that Steal Your Joy is, in a way, a personal book, born out of my own experiences. I hadn't been on this earth very many years when it began to sink in that lots of things were not going to go my way. I'd get all excited about a plan or an event that was on the horizon of my life, when suddenly things didn't pan out and my spirit would hit rock bottom with a mighty thud. There was always a thief waiting in the wings to steal my joy and enthusiasm. I hated that. So much so that it finally struck me (sort of like being run over by a large truck), "How long are you going to live like this, Luci? How long are you going to let life sit on top of you with its disappointments, anxieties, pressures, and regrets? Why don't you figure out a way to beat life at its own game?"

That's when I decided to begin dwelling on the positive instead of the negative. That's when celebrating life became a conscious choice, a decision to live fully, every day and in every way, to the degree that I was able. That's when I realized that the presence of God could actually enter into my circumstances and change things for the better. And, oh, what a difference that change in attitude has made in the way I face life!

Believe it or not, we all have many reasons to celebrate life in spite of the situations in which we find ourselves. Today. This minute. There is something—some perk—in your life that is cause for celebration. Think about it. Start this way: "[Look] at the hour before you, with its myriad demands, plans, concerns, and problems and [ask] God, in the midst of all that, to give you a perk—just for the love of life . . . no other reason."[1] We all lead such busy, stressful lives. We feel overwhelmed. We experience pressure and nagging deadlines that drive us crazy. To celebrate anything for any reason would never enter our thinking. But believe me, we need those perks to keep going. They sweeten the bitter tastes of life.

The highest and most desirable state of the soul is to praise God in celebration for being alive. Without perks our lives are easily lost in the world of money, machines, anxieties, or inertia. Our poor, splendid souls! How they fight for food! They have forgotten how to celebrate. They have forgotten how to request little perks. Our hurried, stressful, busy lives are unquestionably the most dangerous enemy of celebrating life itself. Somehow, we must learn how to achieve momentary slowdowns, and request from God a heightened awareness of the conception that life is a happy thing, a festival to be enjoyed rather than a drudgery to be endured. Life is *full* of perks if we train our souls to perceive them, ". . . a thousand tiny things from which one can weave a bright necklace of little pleasures for one's life."[2]

It is my desire in this book to encourage you to take up celebrating life as a full-time occupation. Consciously. I believe we can be taught to do that. Celebrate everything under the sun. Celebrate you: your talents; your experiences; your uniqueness. Celebrate relationships: with friends; family; colleagues; God. Celebrate the past and the present. Celebrate where you've come from—your progress. Count your blessings and celebrate them. Celebrate the thrill of learning and broadening your viewpoint on various issues. Did you know you can even celebrate your trials and difficulties? This guide shows you how.
When we get into this mindset, living takes on a brand new feeling. There's praise instead of blame or complaint. Joy instead of sorrow. Acceptance in place of rejection. Even peace where there was once anxiety. It works!

But, it doesn't happen overnight. Learning to be grateful no matter what comes our way and being able to celebrate it takes time and effort. It's a process. This guide, I hope, will aid you in that process.

You can work through these lessons alone to great benefit. You may gain even more from them, however, if you participate in a small group that works through them together. We can all learn much from the experiences of others, and there's a lot of support to be gained in group fellowship. Experience also shows that in putting lessons learned into practice, we do much better if we feel accountable to others—if we know someone will ask us periodically how we're doing at putting our good intentions into action.

Each of the eight lessons is divided into six sections:

1. *An opening quote,* either from one of my books, or one written especially for this guide. My goal here is to plunge you quickly into the topic at hand and get your mental and emotional wheels turning.

2. *Identifying Your Blocks.* Here you'll be asked to consider those areas in your life that hold you back, those areas that block you from positive thinking and living. You'll begin to discover why you may not be celebrating as much as you'd like to.

3. *Raising Your Sights.* Next, a Bible study is provided so you can discover where you stand in light of God's Word. (This is one of the most fun elements of each lesson. Each time I dig in here I see something new myself.) Knowing God's Word as it relates to each topic can give you insight, hope, and determination as you make decisions to celebrate each day.

4. *Opening Your Mind.* Here, all sorts of quotations have been gathered to broaden your point of view. In addition to some of my comments here and there, I'm sharing with you the thoughts of many of my favorite authors—those who have helped mold my thinking in certain arenas and shown me alternatives to my own limited viewpoints. Truly, they have opened my mind. You may not agree with everything they have to say; in fact, they may pull you way outside of your comfort zone. All the better! And if you're doing this study with a group, this section may spark some great discussions.

5. *Charting Your Course.* Next, you'll be requested to become a bit philosophical and, at times, transparent about actual situations that perhaps you've never considered celebrating. You'll take a personal inventory of sorts, and gain a vision for how you can move from where you are to where you'd like to be as a person who celebrates well. (We're getting into the nitty-gritty here!)

6. *Choosing to Celebrate.* Finally, the choice is yours to take all this information you've pondered, written, studied, and even confessed, and put it to work for you as you begin celebrating throughout even the hidden areas of your life.

The benefits? Well, I can promise that if you start this study and consistently follow it through to the end, you'll experience a noticeable difference in daily living. Your circumstances may take a while to change (and cheer up! some may never change), but YOU will change. You'll grow. You'll mellow out. You'll feel better about yourself, your burdens, and your relationships. You'll become more accepting of yourself and your circumstances. You'll see things through different eyes. Most important, you'll celebrate your faith and your Lord in a whole new way.

So get your plan of attack ready. You're about to catch a bunch of thieves!

NOTES
1. Luci Swindoll, *You Bring the Confetti* (Dallas, Tex.: Word, Inc., 1986), page 13.
2. Swindoll, page 13.

NOTE TO DISCUSSION LEADERS

Each of the eight lessons in this guide contains significantly more material than it's possible to cover in one group discussion session. The lessons have been designed to take the individual reader deeply into the topic at hand, to the extent that he or she cares to explore deeply. If members of your group complete each lesson in its entirety during the week, they will be likely to grasp and apply the deepest truths about celebrating life. They will also have significant insights to contribute to a group discussion that will necessarily be more superficial because of its brevity. Therefore, you should encourage group members to complete each lesson on their own between meetings.

To help you as the group leader stimulate and direct effective group discussion, eight or nine questions from each lesson are listed below. These questions will get at the heart of the lesson and foster the most interesting, balanced, and profitable discussion.

> Lesson 1—1, 2, 10, 12, 14, 16, 21, 23
> Lesson 2—3, 6, 8, 10, 11, 14, 18, 20
> Lesson 3—1, 2, 5, 8, 11, 13, 17, 18
> Lesson 4—2, 3, 4, 6, 9, 10, 12, 15
> Lesson 5—1, 2, 8, 12, 14, 15, 17, 22, 25
> Lesson 6—2, 4, 6, 12, 15, 17, 21, 22
> Lesson 7—2, 3, 5, 6, 12, 14, 16, 19, 20
> Lesson 8—1, 2, 5, 7, 9, 10, 13, 19

Each week (or at whatever intervals your group convenes) you might also want to allot a few minutes for group members to share how they have applied the previous lesson in the week just passed.

It will ultimately be up to you to determine the number and type of questions your group discusses, depending on its size, make-up, and time frame. Relax and enjoy the group process. Make it a celebration!

CELEBRATING THE PRESENT:
Catching Discontent

To experience happiness we must train ourselves to live in this moment, to savor it for what it is, not running ahead in anticipation of some future date nor lagging behind in the paralysis of the past. With wholeness and sensitivity we must live in the here and now. "But what if I don't like the here and now?" you ask. "What if my present moment is one of disappointment or impairment or heartache? How then do I savor that moment?" Good questions. And the answers reside in the first and most profound principle in the art of savoring life. Pleasure lies in the heart, not in the happenstance. Our circumstances may be dreadful and riddled with reasons for discouragement or sorrow, but that doesn't mean those moments are utterly devoid of happiness.[1]

Identifying Your Blocks

1. What is your definition of happiness?

   TO B able to share that day on any day to share it with someone

2. Do you believe it's possible to be happy even when circumstances are less than ideal? Why or why not?

   yes

3. a. On the scale below, indicate how consistently you have enjoyed and celebrated life regardless of your circumstances during the past five years.

1 (2) 3 4 5 6 7 8 9 10
Very inconsistently   Very consistently

b. Has your capacity to celebrate increased or decreased through the years? Why?

decreased - well the kids it was my job ect.

c. Has there been a period of time in your life when you celebrated more or less? What was happening during that time?

When I was younger and when I lived with my mom.

4. a. What are some situations or attitudes in your life that produce discontent?

When I which is usually always think of the past.

b. How do those things keep you from being happy?

just remember the evil I had

5. Is it difficult for you to fully live in and savor the "here and now" in your life? If so, why?

yes, because its seems I can't let go of the past

Raising Your Sights

6. a. Read Exodus 16:14-20. Why do you think some of the Israelites hoarded the manna God provided?

   b. What lessons do you suppose God wanted to teach them by providing only enough manna for their needs and no more? *so this wouldn't want to always take more than they needed.*

7. Read 2 Corinthians 11:23-29. What things did Paul experience as an apostle of Christ?

8. a. According to Philippians 4:11-13, what was Paul's attitude toward the circumstances in his life?

   b. What important truth does he reveal in verse 11 about the development of contentment?

   c. In verse 12 Paul refers to a "secret" he has learned about being content. What do you think that secret is?

9. a. Read 1 Timothy 6:6-10. What do you think is the "great gain" Paul refers to in verse 6? Why is it so valuable?

b. Verse 7 provides a perspective that produces contentment. What is that perspective? Why does it help?

c. What are the potential consequences of discontent?

d. Have you loved money? If so, what are some ways the love of money has led to discontent or grief in your life?

e. Besides money, what are some other things on which you have banked your happiness?

f. Have these things brought you lasting contentment? Why or why not?

10. a. In 1 Timothy 6:17, Paul says God provides us with everything for our enjoyment. Have you found this to be true
in your life? On what evidence do you base your answer?

   b. What kind of provision from God do you think Paul is
   referring to?

11. a. What reasons do the following verses give for trusting in
God?

   2 Chronicles 32:7-8

   Psalm 9:10

   b. We are told in Psalm 118:8-9 to put our confidence in
   the Lord rather than in people. Why is God (who can't
   be seen) more worthy of our trust than human beings
   (who can be seen)?

   c. Has anything happened in your life to bear out the truth
   of these verses? If so, what was it?

12. a. In Matthew 6:34, Jesus urges us to live in the present.
What is His rationale?

b. What is the benefit of living in the present?

Opening Your Mind

One way to combat immobilization, however slight, is to learn to live in the present moment. Present-moment living, getting in touch with your "now," is at the heart of effective living. When you think about it, there really is no other moment you can ever live. Now is all there is, and the future is just another present moment to live when it arrives. One thing is certain; you cannot live it until it does appear.[2]

◆

Each of us is surrounded by opportunities to become excited and involved in activities at hand. But we're waiting for the other shoe to drop. We're wanting things to get better, to lighten up, to go away. We're waiting for a ship to come in that never went out.[3]

◆

God's plan for you is not past tense or hidden in the obscurity of the future. It is continuous. God's will is always current. It is for this you have been brought into the kingdom: to live this day, within its circumstances, in obedience. To stretch out in the fact of His security and be willing to become. To celebrate His presence even in flight. God has a plan for you. It's current. Celebrate it! Now![4]

◆

When religion has said its last word, there is little that we need other than God Himself. The evil habit of seeking God-and effectively prevents us from finding God in full revelation. In the and lies our great woe. If we omit the and we shall soon find God, and in Him we shall find that for which we have all our lives been secretly longing.[5]

◆

Life passes like a flash of lightning whose blaze barely lasts long enough to see. While the earth and the sky stand still forever, how swiftly changing time flies across man's face. O you who sit over your full cup and do not drink, tell me, whom are you still waiting for?[6]

◆

The decision to set the mind on the higher things of life is an act of the will. That is why celebration is a Discipline. It is not something that falls on our head. It is the result of a consciously chosen way of thinking and living. As we choose that way, the healing and redemption in Christ will break into the inner recesses of our lives and relationships, and the inevitable relationship will be joy [7]

Charting Your Course

13. a. In the past week, what were some ways you celebrated—in attitude or action?

b. Describe some of your circumstances in the past week.

14. What does it mean to you to celebrate? If you had a full day to celebrate just as you want to, what would you do?

15. Do you feel yourself waiting for things to get better before you celebrate the "now"? If so, what feelings or circumstances do you feel need to change before you can be content?

16. a. Think of someone you know who seems to be content regardless of his or her circumstances. What do you suppose is that person's "secret"?

  b. What can you learn about celebrating life by observing him or her?

Choosing to Celebrate

17. Name five accomplishments, experiences, or changes in your life from the past year that you're happy about.

18. What are three things you're thankful for right at this moment?

19. a. Think about someone you care about and write down *only* the things you appreciate about that person today.

b. Do the same for yourself. What do you like about *you*?

20. Name at least ten reasons why your life is worth living today.

21. Paraphrase in your own words my statement, "Pleasure lies in the heart, not in the happenstance."

22. What one verse from the "Raising Your Sights" section of this lesson most encourages you to be content in your circumstances? Write it down on an index card and place it where you'll see it several times today.

23. What one statement or concept from the "Opening Your Mind" section most challenges or helps you? Why?

24. In the week ahead, what is one basic way you can act on the truth you've learned?

NOTES
1. Luci Swindoll, *You Bring the Confetti* (Dallas, Tex.: Word, Inc., 1986), page 17.
2. Wayne W. Dyer, *Your Erroneous Zones* (New York: Funk & Wagnalls, 1976), pages 20-21.
3. Luci Swindoll, *After You've Dressed for Success* (Dallas, Tex.: Word, Inc., 1987), page 29.
4. Jeannette Clift George, *Travel Tips from a Reluctant Traveler* (Nashville: Thomas Nelson Publishers, 1987), page 171.
5. A.W. Tozer, *The Pursuit of God* (Camp Hill, Pa.: Christian Publications, Inc., 1982), page 18.
6. Hermann Hesse, *Klingsor's Last Summer* (New York: Farrar, Straus and Giroux, 1970), page 166.
7. Richard J. Foster, *Celebration of Discipline* (New York: Harper & Row, Publishers, Inc., 1978, 1988), pages 166-167.

CELEBRATING THE PAST:
Catching Regret

We all know that when the future arrives it becomes the present: Now. By the same token, all of our nows will soon be the past: Then. It's the cycle of life, from cradle to grave. That's why the present is so important. It's what makes up both our past and our future. When we seize our moments, savor them, and put them to good use, we rarely have regrets. Yet, there are countless people out there living in regret, especially older people. "Regrets are the natural properties of gray hairs," wrote Charles Dickens. But why does that have to be so?

God's Word gives us permission to be happy now. To live fully now. To value life now. To grow. To change. To risk. To accept. In fact, because He is our forerunner, He paves the way for our present and future. It is He who enables us to move along steadily in the right direction. It is He who makes all things—even what we think are mistakes or oversights—beautiful in His time. Herein lies the secret of having no sorrow over what we've done in the past, or more important, what we left undone. He releases us from those debilitating feelings that hold us back from living life and celebrating every moment to the hilt.

Identifying Your Blocks

1. Indicate how often you experience guilt or regret over past events or failures of which you've repented.

1	2	3	4	5	6	7	8	9	10
Never									Very often

2. a. As you think back over events of the past week, is there anything you wish you could change? If so, what?

my attitude of being so lonley

   b. If you were able to go back and change that thing, how do you think your circumstances or feelings would be different today?

I don't think it would still be feeling so lonely

3. Which of the following hinder you in your ability to fully accept and celebrate your past?

____ Difficulty accepting God's forgiveness
____ Difficulty forgiving yourself
____ Difficulty believing God can use everything in your life for the highest good
✗ Believing things would have worked out better if you'd only tried harder
____ Resentment toward people who have hurt you or limited your options
____ Resentment toward God for the things He's allowed to happen

____ Other _____

Raising Your Sights

4. a. Read Isaiah 30:15-17. In verse 15, the Hebrew word for salvation refers to freedom, safety, and victory. The Hebrew word for strength also means victory. What did God say is the way to experience salvation and strength?

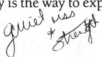

quiet rest & strength

   b. In your own words, explain the Israelites' response to God's offer.

c. In what ways have you refused God's offer of safety and victory? What "horses" have you used to assist you in controlling your own life? *the past*

d. Do you regularly practice repentance, rest, and trust? If not, why not?

e. How can accepting God's offer help you enjoy life more fully, with a sense of celebration? *+ tired*

5. a. Read Hebrews 10:5-23. In your own words, explain why we can have confidence in God's presence.

b. If Christ's sacrifice has opened a new way into God's presence, what was the old way (see verses 5-14)?

c. As you think about your life, which covenant do you seem to be living under: the old or the new? How do you know?

d. Verse 23 tells us why we can live confidently and guilt-free. What is that reason?

6. What do the following passages say about God's willing-ness to forgive us in spite of our failures? Write down the key thought that strikes you in each passage.

Psalm 78:34-39

Psalm 103:8-14

Psalm 106:39-45

Isaiah 57:15-18

Micah 7:18-20

7. a. What does John 3:17 say was Christ's purpose in coming to earth?

b. What was *not* His purpose?

8. What do the following verses say is the prerequisite to receiving God's forgiveness?

2 Chronicles 7:14

Isaiah 55:7

Acts 3:19

9. According to the following verses, what is the primary reason God forgives us: Psalm 106:7-8, Isaiah 48:8-11, Ezekiel 36:22-23?

10. a. What do you believe the difference is between a sin and a mistake? How do you know?

    b. Whether you sin or err, how do the following verses encourage you?

    Proverbs 19:21

    Romans 8:28-39

11. a. If you resent someone for hurting you, how does that grudge keep you from fully celebrating your past?

    b. How can the truth of the following verses free you from holding onto your anger?

    Proverbs 20:22

    Romans 12:19

    Ephesians 4:31-32

Opening Your Mind

A lifetime is just too short for us to spend it accumulating regrets for what we might have done. We need to remind ourselves and especially our children, that death is nothing to fear as long as we understand that each moment has a life unto itself with as much possibility for joy and happiness as we are willing to bring to it. [1]

◆

For we cannot climb into a time machine, become that long-gone child and get what we want when we oh so desperately wanted it. The days for that getting are over, finished, done. We have needs we can meet in different ways, in better ways, in ways that create new experience. But until we can . . . let go of [the] past, we are doomed to repeat it. [2]

◆

If you cannot free people from their wrongs and see them as the needy people they are, you enslave yourself to your own painful past, and by fastening yourself to the past, you let hate become your future. You can reverse your future only by releasing other people from their pasts. [3]

◆

My security as a believer isn't in the strength of my faith. Nor in the validity of my doctrine. Not even in how many Bible verses I know. All that is wonderful, but my security as a believer rests in His grip on me. God will not relax His grip! *I've known times when that grip hurt, times when that grip prevented me from running along a self-chosen path, and times when that grip caused me to let go the hold I had on something outside God's will. That grip hasn't always been comfortable, but that grip has been my security.* [4]

◆

Wisdom is the acquired ability to live life well. It's living life against the grindstone and coming away polished instead of being chewed up. It's when our mistakes and failures become our teachers. . . . Often the hard way can be the very best way to make sure you never forget. Sin that's been confessed, wrestled with, and

*overcome is one of the finest teachers we have. Our struggles and
defeats can increase our spiritual growth just as much as our
victories—if we learn from them. . . . How can anyone grow
through temptations, trials, and even the ravages of deep sin? We
can all grow through the scars and brokenness because of the counsel, comfort, and healing of the God who uses all things—yes, even
the desolate aftermath following sin—to bring us back to our spiritual senses and back to Him.*[5]

◆

*As you look back on your life, much the way Tolstoy's Ivan
Ilych did, you'll find that you seldom experience regret for anything
that you've done. It is what you haven't done that will torment you.
The message, therefore, is clear. Do it! Develop an appreciation for
the present moment. Seize every second of your life and savor it.
Value your present moments.*[6]

◆

*Whatever time is assigned to each to live, with that he ought to
be content . . . for a short period of life is long enough for living well
and honorably, and if you should advance further, you need no more
grieve than farmers do when the loveliness of springtime has passed,
that summer and autumn have come.*

*If . . . God should grant me that from this period of life I should
become a child again and cry in the cradle I should earnestly refuse
it, nor in truth should I like, having run, as it were, my course, to be
called back to the starting place from the goal.*

*Neither do I regret that I have lived, since I have lived in such a
way that I conceive I was not born in vain, and from this life I depart
as from a temporary lodging, not as from a home, for nature has
assigned us to it as an inn to sojourn in, not a place of habitation.*[7]

Charting Your Course

12. Is there anything in your past that you feel will prevent God
    from working out His perfect in your life? What makes
    you think that?

13. a. Is there any sin in your past for which you have not repented? If so, what is it?

    b. Will you repent of it now? If something is blocking you, what is it?

    c. If you repent, can you let go of your guilt and regret? Why or why not?

14. How do you think God feels about you regardless of your imperfections? How do you know?

15. a. If you still feel resentment toward yourself, others, or God because of past events in your life, explain why.

    b. What do you think God would say to you about your response?

Choosing to Celebrate

16. a. Review your answer to question 2 in the "Identifying Your Blocks" section of this lesson. Does what you've learned so far affect that response? Why or why not?

b. In light of Romans 8:28-31, try to identify at least three ways God has used the event or failure you wrote about. (If you're still too close to that event, answer this question in regard to an event further back in your past.)

c. How do you feel about that event in light of what God has done with it?

d. Answer the same series of questions in regard to a hurt you suffered because of someone else's sin or mistake.

17. a. What do you feel is the worst thing you've ever done?

b. If you feel any guilt over that action, spend some time in prayer, asking God to tell you what He thinks about you and your failure. What is His response to you?

18. a. Next time you feel guilt or regret over actions you've repented of, what will you do?

    b. What will you do next time you feel anger or resentment toward others?

19. What one verse in the "Raising Your Sights" section of this lesson encourages or challenges you most? Try memorizing this verse this week so you can recall it when you need it.

20. a. Do you believe my statement, "God's Word gives us permission to be happy now"? Why or why not?

    b. If you can, write out on a separate piece of paper a few paragraphs on the subject of "Why I Can Celebrate My Past."

NOTES
1. Leo Buscaglia, *Bus 9 to Paradise* (Thorofare, N.J.: SLACK, Inc./William Morrow & Co., 1986), page 271.
2. Judith Viorst, *Necessary Losses* (New York: Fawcett Gold Medal, 1986), page 79.
3. Lewis B. Smedes, *Forgive & Forget* (New York: Simon & Schuster, Inc., 1984), page 47.
4. Jeannette Clift George, *Travel Tips from a Reluctant Traveler* (Nashville: Thomas Nelson Publishers, 1987), page 71.
5. David Swartz, *Dancing with Broken Bones* (Colorado Springs, Colo.: NavPress, 1987), pages 65, 67-68.
6. Wayne W. Dyer, *Your Erroneous Zones* (New York: Funk & Wagnalls, 1976), pages 22-23.
7. Helen Hayes, *A Gift of Joy* (Greenwich, Conn.: Fawcett Publications, 1965), pages 208-209.

CELEBRATING PROGRESS:
Catching Perfectionism

Sometimes it's tough to be me because I don't like me. I'm disappointed in me. I'm embarrassed at the way I look, or I'm not being understood and affirmed by somebody I want to love me. Clearly, without doubt, there is nothing wrong with seeking to change in ourselves what is able to be changed (I'm a strong advocate of that). But the essence of who we are—our age, our sex, our looks, our past, our shortcomings, our broken promises to ourselves, our unfulfilled dreams—we must learn to live with and to accept for what is. We must seek to walk in God's light and in His counsel, realizing that contentment, acceptance, love, compassion, vulnerability, and charm are the by-products of an intimate relationship with Him, not the results of conforming to the mandates and demands of an insatiable world. . . . Simply put, it takes getting outside ourselves and creating what is not, balanced and blended with getting inside ourselves and accepting what is. [1]

Identifying Your Blocks

1. Do you consider yourself to be a perfectionist? What evidence can you give to support your answer?

2. a. On the scale below, indicate how completely you accept yourself at this stage in your life.

   1   2   3   4   5   6   7   8   9   10

   No   Total
   acceptance   acceptance

   b. How often do you worry about where you are in relation to where you think you should be?

   1   2   3   4   5   6   7   8   9   10

   Always   Never

   c. How do you usually respond to the imperfections in your life?

   ____ Try harder to change.
   ____ Pray for change.
   ____ Try to ignore imperfections.
   ____ Trust God's timetable.
   ____ Berate self.
   ____ Blame circumstances.
   ____ Quietly grumble or fret.
   ____ Blame others.
   ____ Give up in discouragement.
   ____ Ask others for advice.
   ____ Peacefully accept imperfection.

   ____ Other_____

3. a. Which areas in your life do you feel need the most improvement? Number them in sequence (with 1 needing the most improvement).

   ____ vocational   ____ financial
   ____ relational   ____ physical
   ____ spiritual   ____ personal (character)
   ____ emotional
   ____ intellectual   ____ other(s) _____

b. As you think about the need for progress, what do you feel? (Check all that apply.)

____ determination   ____ peace
____ pessimism   ____ confidence
____ sadness   ____ excitement
____ pressure   ____ hope
____ self-contempt   ____ anger
____ frustration   ____ other _____

c. How does your assessment of your progress help you in or keep you from celebrating life?

Raising Your Sights

1. a. On the scale below, indicate how much control you feel you have over your progress toward becoming the person God has called you to be.

1   2   3   4   5   6   7   8   9   10
No control   Total control

b. What do the following verses have to say about your control over your journey through life?

Proverbs 27:1

Jeremiah 10:23

John 15:5

2 Corinthians 3:4-5

c. How would you put the central truth of these verses in your own words?

5. What *are* we responsible for regarding our progress? Record the central thought in each of the following passages.

Psalm 84:5-7

Micah 7:7-8

Galatians 5:4-5,16

Hebrews 6:11-12

Hebrews 10:35-36

Hebrews 12:1-2

6. a. Read Philippians 3:12-14. What three things did Paul do as he lived on this side of Heaven and without the perfection he would someday experience?

b. What two reasons do verses 15-16 give for why we can be at peace no matter where we are in our journey?

7. Paul made three other statements that can give us confidence at all times. Summarize them in your own words.

Philippians 1:6

Philippians 2:13

1 Thessalonians 5:23-24

8. a. What do the following verses say God will do for you?

Psalm 32:8

Psalm 73:24

Isaiah 30:19-21

Isaiah 42:16

Isaiah 58:11

b. How would you summarize the central truth of the above verses in a one-sentence promise?

9. The following verses describe a cause and effect relationship between our action and God's response. Read the
verses and fill in the chart.

IF I WILL . . .	GOD WILL . . .
Proverbs 3:5-6	
Isaiah 26:3	
Philippians 4:6-7	

Opening Your Mind

*We have an idea that God is leading us to a particular end, a desired
goal; He is not. The question of getting to a particular end is a mere
incident. What we call the process, God calls the end. What is my
dream of God's purpose? His purpose is that I depend on Him and
on His power now. If I can stay in the middle of the turmoil calm and
unperplexed, that is the end of the purpose of God. God is not working towards a particular finish; His end is the process—that I see
Him walking on the waves, no shore in sight, no success, no goal,
just the absolute certainty that it is all right because I see Him walking on the sea. It is the process, not the end, which is glorifying to
God.*[2]

◆

*Would that there were an award for people who come to
understand the concept of enough. Good enough. Successful*

*enough. Thin enough. Rich enough. . . . When you have self-respect
you have enough, and when you have enough, you have
self-respect.*[3]

◆

*Many of us fail to celebrate in our travels throughout life
because we deny the process. . . . God may take us in His grace from
Monday to Friday, but we'll go through Tuesday, Wednesday, and
Thursday to get there. These days, you can be sure, will be packed
full of choices and deliberations, losings and winnings, all sorts of
events that will be part of the processing of our week. Even though I
have been a reluctant traveler, I can vouch for the certainty of God's
unwavering fellowship, the sovereign promise of His itinerary, and
His limitless patience with people in process.*[4]

◆

*We have to do our part. But I believe we can and will do our
part best by doing it one day at a time. If it's time to do something,
we'll know. If it's time for something to happen, it will. Trust ourselves and God. . . . I've never yet reached a goal or solved a problem that has enabled me to live happily ever after. Life goes on, and I
try to live happily and peacefully   Things happen when the time
is right—when we're ready, when God is ready, when the world is
ready. Give up. Let go. But keep it on our list.*[5]

◆

*In many people's minds, change must be nearly complete, at
least dramatic, or it doesn't count. And the change required to con-
vince us we've found the secret of growth must be the change we
want the most. . . .*

*Evangelicals sometimes expect too much or, to put it more pre-
cisely, we look for a kind of change God hasn't promised. . . . We
manage to interpret biblical teaching to support our longing for perfection. As a result, we measure our progress by standards we will
never meet until Heaven. . . .*

*We therefore claim God's power as the guarantee of total
change from pressure to peace, from disappointment to joy—and
then live with an intolerable burden that either crushes us with
despair or requires us to pretend we're better than we are. . . .*

*We will, of course, be flawless—one day. . . . But for now,
struggles continue. There is a necessary pain of living in this world
that we must simply accept.*[6]

◆

*It takes courage to look back down the road to see how far we
have come toward daylight. But the rewards are great. When we give
ourselves credit for all the progress, desire, and willingness to investigate the dark corners of our souls, we have good cause to celebrate
who we are!*

*Facing up to and facing down the demons of guilt and low self-
esteem require great courage. And when we can look not only back-
ward but forward—our task is more courageous still.*

*It's not where we came from, or even where we are, that tells
the story. It's where we're headed that gives rise to hope and the
joyous shout, "I'm getting there! I'm doing just fine!"*[7]

Charting Your Course

10. a. Review your response to question 3a in the "Identifying
Your Blocks" section of this lesson. Over the past five
years, in which area have you seen the most progress?
The least?

b. In each of the areas you ranked as needing the most
improvement, what specific improvements do you feel
need to be made?

11. Review your response to part b of question 3. Has your response changed at all as a result of doing this lesson so far? If so, in what way? If not, why not?

12. a. How often do you consciously celebrate—in attitude or action—your progress and accomplishments?

1	2	3	4	5	6	7	8	9	10
Never									Always

   b. What keeps you from celebrating your progress even more than you do?

13. a. As you reflect on the things you think need changing in your life, do you feel pressure? If so, from what source(s) does this pressure seem to come? Rank them in descending order.

   ___ God
   ___ circumstances
   ___ other people
   ___ self
   ___ other _____

   b. Have you uncovered any truth in this lesson so far that can help relieve that pressure? If so, what is it and how can it help?

Choosing to Celebrate

14. Think again about the area of your life in which you've seen the most progress over the past five years. Plan a way to celebrate that progress and do it in the week ahead. (If you have trouble coming up with a way to celebrate, the following suggestions may help.)

    ▶ Write a letter of thanksgiving to God.
    ▶ Make a list of how your progress has affected your life or the people in your life.
    ▶ Light candles at the breakfast table.
    ▶ Buy yourself something.
    ▶ Sit down and listen to your favorite piece of music.
    ▶ Spend half a day doing *only* what you want to do.
    ▶ Hug yourself.
    ▶ Start a journal by recording this area of progress.

15. List at least five things you have learned about yourself, God, or life as a result of failure or slow progress.

16. Think about the area of your life that needs the most improvement. Spend some time thanking God for this area, telling Him what it has taught you, how you have experienced His faithfulness in spite of it, and what you believe will happen in the future when you take Him at His Word.

17. List at least five reasons why worry is an inappropriate response to the imperfections you see in your life.

18. In light of what you've learned in this lesson, describe the ideal way to respond no matter where you are on your journey through life. Include as many elements as you can draw from the "Raising Your Sights" section.

19. a. Choose one verse from this lesson that particularly encourages or challenges you. Why is this verse so meaningful? Try memorizing it this week.

   b. Specifically, how can you apply the truth of this verse in your life this week?

NOTES
1. Luci Swindoll, *You Bring the Confetti* (Dallas, Tex.: Word, Inc., 1986), page 36.
2. Oswald Chambers, *My Utmost for His Highest* (New York: Dodd, Mead & Company, 1935), page 210.
3. Gail Sheehy, *Passages* (New York: Bantam Books, 1984), page 513.
4. Jeannette Clift George, *Travel Tips from a Reluctant Traveler* (Nashville: Thomas Nelson Publishers, 1987), pages 22-23.
5. Melody Beattie, *Codependent No More* (New York: Harper & Row, Publishers, Inc., 1987), pages 159-160.
6. Larry Crabb, *Inside Out* (Colorado Springs, Colo.: NavPress, 1988), pages 189-190.
7. Earnie Larsen & Carol Larsen Hegarty, *Days of Healing, Days of Joy* (New York: Harper & Row, Publishers, Inc., 1987), March 8.

CELEBRATING TRIALS:
Catching Resentment

Often we find ourselves terrified at the turmoils of human life—we want to stop the world and get off. I've said before that if there were just a little booth attached to the side of the world where I could go and sit and think and pray and wait until this or that problem is over, I'd be so much happier. Then, when I was better and stronger, I'd come back into real life. But it doesn't work that way. And if it did, I'd never grow. I'd never learn. The way I learn is in the midst of the turmoil, because it's not the little booth that calls out my resourceful best; it's the turmoil. Difficult times give me spiritual insight and a chance to trust God, even though that certainly may not be my choice. They pave my way toward endurance, focus, responsibility . . . and courage.[1]

Identifying Your Blocks

1. a. What was the most recent trial you experienced? How did it turn out?

   b. How did you feel when it came? (Check all that apply.)

   ___ resentful   ___ accepting
   ___ anxious   ___ depressed
   ___ panicked   ___ hopeful
   ___ joyful   ___ curious
   ___ peaceful   ___ angry
   ___ resigned   ___ other _____

c. What did you do in response to the trial?

d. What, if anything, did you learn through it?

2. a. Why do you think God allows us to suffer?

b. How do you feel about what you just wrote?

3. Do you feel that trials are a blessing, a curse, or something in between? Why?

Raising Your Sights

4. According to the following verses, what are the intended results of suffering and how are we to respond to them?

RESULT	RESPONSE
2 Corinthians 4:7-11,16-18	
Hebrews 12:5-11	

RESULT	RESPONSE
James 1:2-4	
1 Peter 1:6-7	

5. What promises do the following verses hold out for you?

Isaiah 41:17

Jeremiah 29:11-14

Romans 8:17-18

1 Peter 4:12-13

1 Peter 5:10

6. Read Philippians 2:5-11 and Hebrews 12:2-4. How does Christ's example encourage or challenge you in your own suffering?

7. a. According to Isaiah 50:10-11, what are we to do when we're in distress?

   b. What are we *not* to do?

   c. Describe the last time you "lit your own fire" rather than relied on God when hard times came.

   d. Thinking back over past trials, what are some other ways you depended on your own resources instead of on God?

8. According to the following verses, what can we count on when we trust God in the midst of our pain?

   Psalm 27:13-14

   Psalm 42:11

   Psalm 46:1-3,10

   Psalm 55:22

   Psalm 57:1-2

Psalm 71:1,20-21

Psalm 112:1,7-8

Lamentations 3:19-33

9. a. Trials have a hidden blessing not only for us, but for others. In fact, according to 2 Corinthians 1:3-7, that blessing is on-going as long as we live. What is it?

b. Have you experienced this blessing? If so, how?

Opening Your Mind

Just keep in mind when you come up against irksome barriers, that they are designed to build character, not destroy it. The problem is, we tend to want our troublesome situations changed now. We're sick of the obstacles and we want them out of the way immediately. But that's just not the way most problems are solved. More often, change comes by facing one day at a time. . . . Sometimes we get the blues over roadblocks. And not only the blues, but downright discouragement. We want to look at the world and say, "Don't nobody bring me no bad news. I can't take it. I'm sick of it. One more piece of it will do me in!" But there are ways around; there is strength to go through "bad news." And one way is to do things minute by minute, one day at a time.[2]

◆

*We can confront our problems without searching frantically for
an exit from reality. Our pain is what teaches us the things we need
to know. By being willing to be broken, we are able to become whole.
Through our distress, we are watched over by the One who heals us.
We need no exit.*[3]

◆

*Suffering only hurts because you fear it. Suffering only hurts
because you complain about it. It pursues you only because you flee
from it. You must not flee, you must not complain, you must not
fear. You must love. You know all this yourself, you know quite well,
deep within you, that there is only a single magic, a single power, a
single salvation, and a single happiness, and that is called loving.
Well then, love your suffering. Do not resist it, do not flee from it.
Taste how sweet it is in its essence, give yourself to it, do not meet it
with aversion. It is only your aversion that hurts, nothing else. Sorrow is not sorrow, death is not death if you do not make them so!
Suffering is magnificent music—the moment you give ear to it. But
you never listen to it; you always have a different, private, stubborn
music and melody in your ear which you will not relinquish and with
which the music of suffering will not harmonize. Listen to me! Listen
to me, and remember: suffering is nothing, suffering is illusion. Only
you yourself create it, only you cause yourself pain! . . . Just suffer,
my son, just suffer and drain the cup to the dregs! The harder you
try to avoid it, the bitterer the drink will be. The coward drinks his
fate like poison or medicine, you must drink yours like wine and fire.
Then it will taste sweet.*[4]

◆

*This call [to spiritual consecration] has nothing to do with per-
sonal sanctification, but with being made broken bread and poured-
out wine. God can never make us wine if we object to the fingers He
uses to crush us with. If God would only use His own fingers, and
make me broken bread and poured-out wine in a special way! But
when He uses someone whom we dislike, or some set of circumstances to which we said we would never submit, and makes those
the crushers, we object. We must never choose the scene of our own
martyrdom. If ever we are going to be made into wine, we will have*

*to be crushed; you cannot drink grapes. Grapes become wine only
when they have been squeezed.* [5]

◆

*A popular teaching today instructs us to praise God for the var-
ious difficulties that come into our lives, asserting that there is great
transforming power in thus praising God. In its best form such teaching is a way of encouraging us to look up the road a bit through the
eye of faith and see what will be. It affirms in our hearts the joyful
assurance that God takes all things and works them for the good of
those who love Him. In its worst form this teaching denies the vile-
ness of evil and baptizes the most horrible tragedies as the will of
God. Scripture commands us to live in a spirit of thanksgiving in the
midst of all situations; it does not command us to celebrate the presence of evil.* [6]

◆

*And a woman spoke, saying, Tell us of pain. And he said: Your
pain is the breaking of the shell that encloses your understanding.
Even as the stone of the fruit must break, that its heart may stand in
the sun, so must you know pain. And could you keep your heart in
wonder at the daily miracles of your life, your pain would seem less
wondrous than your joy; and you would accept the seasons of your
heart, even as you have always accepted the seasons that pass over
your fields. And you would watch with serenity through the winters
of your grief.*

*Much of your pain is self-chosen. It is the bitter potion by
which the physician within you heals your sick self. Therefore trust
the physician, and drink his remedy in silence and tranquility; for his
hand, though heavy and hard, is guided by the tender hand of the
Unseen, and the cup he brings, though it burn your lips, has been
fashioned of the clay which the Potter has moistened with His own
sacred tears.* [7]

◆

*God has paid us the intolerable compliment of loving us, in the
deepest, most tragic, most inexorable sense. It is natural for us to
wish that God had designed for us a less glorious and less arduous
destiny: but then we are wishing not for more love but for less.* [8]

Charting Your Course

10. a. How do you feel about the idea of celebrating your suffering?

b. Have you ever consciously embraced and celebrated your trials? If so, in what way?

c. What enabled you to celebrate in spite of your pain?

11. a. On the scale below, indicate how much patience you have generally had in the past as you've endured trials.

1	2	3	4	5	6	7	8	9	10

I had to find a way out.   I could wait peacefully on the Lord.

b. Have you discovered anything in this lesson that you believe will enable you to be more patient during your next trial? If so, what is it?

12. a. What do you want your suffering to produce in your life?

b. Do you have any assurance that this desire will be fulfilled? Why or why not?

Choosing to Celebrate

13. a. Think again of your most recent trial and list at least three reasons why you can be grateful for it.

   b. In what ways did that trial pave your way toward the results I refer to in the opening excerpt?

   Endurance

   Focus

   Responsibility

   Courage

14. a. If you're currently hurting over something, what are at least three reasons for celebration?

   b. Spend some time in prayer, telling God of your pain and then praising Him for your reasons to celebrate.

15. Think of someone you know whose attitude in the midst of suffering has inspired you. What exactly inspires or challenges you? If possible, ask that person about his or her secret. Make a note of the answer and contemplate it in the weeks ahead.

16. Choose one of the quotes from the "Opening Your Mind" section of this lesson and on a separate sheet of paper, write about why it encourages you to celebrate your own suffering.

NOTES

1. Luci Swindoll, *After You've Dressed for Success* (Dallas, Tex.: Word, Inc., 1987), pages 39-40.
2. Swindoll, pages 75-76.
3. *Food for Thought* (Center City, Minn.: Hazelden Foundation, 1980), November 18.
4. Hermann Hesse, *My Belief* (New York: Farrar, Straus and Giroux, 1974), pages 53-55.
5. Oswald Chambers, *My Utmost for His Highest* (New York: Dodd, Mead & Company, 1935), page 274.
6. Richard J. Foster, *Celebration of Discipline* (New York: Harper & Row, Publishers, Inc., 1978, 1988), page 167.
7. Kahlil Gibran, *The Prophet* (New York: Alfred A. Knopf, Inc., 1923), pages 47-48.
8. C.S. Lewis, *The Problem of Pain* (New York: Macmillan Publishing Company, 1962), pages 41,43.

CELEBRATING RELATIONSHIPS:
Catching Self-Protection

I've heard it said, "God's will is people." I believe it. Relationships
with other people are what teach us about living, learning, and loving. In fact, if any investment of energy takes more time than our
relationships, it will more than likely pervert our purpose for being
on this earth as God's people.

There are occasions, of course, when investing in others is one
of the hardest things to do. Deep, sound, meaningful relationships
are hard to maintain because they call out of us something that
makes us transparent and vulnerable. People get under our skin
when we let down our guard. We don't like that. What if they hurt
us? So, we shield ourselves from that possibility by erecting barriers.
We put up a front. We "self-protect." But, what happens if we make
that a lifestyle?

In his book The Four Loves, C.S. Lewis insightfully tells us:
"To love . . . is to be vulnerable. Love anything, and your heart will
certainly be wrung and possibly broken. If you want to make sure of
keeping it intact, you must give it to no one, not even to an animal.
Wrap it carefully around hobbies and little luxuries; avoid all entanglements; lock it up safe in the casket or coffin of your selfishness.
But in that casket—safe, dark, motionless, airless—it will change. It
will not be broken; it will become unbreakable, impenetrable,
irredeemable."[1]

If you ask me, it's much more realistic and enjoyable to run the
risk of being hurt by letting down our guard and learning to celebrate
relationships, no matter what the cost. When we first give our hearts
to Jesus Christ, He shows us how to give them to others.

Identifying Your Blocks

1. a. Name at least five qualities you value in a friend.

   b. Are these qualities different from what you look for in a spouse, a mentor, an employer, or an employee? If so, in what ways?

2. What do you think are the four or five most crucial elements of a healthy close relationship of any kind?

3. Think about your three most important adult relationships. On the scales below, indicate how consistently the elements you listed in question 2 are operating in these relationships.

Person _____

1	2	3	4	5	6	7	8	9	10
Never									Always

Person _____

1	2	3	4	5	6	7	8	9	10
Never									Always

Person _____

1	2	3	4	5	6	7	8	9	10
Never									Always

4. How consistently do you contribute to the growth of these elements in all your relationships?

1   2   3   4   5   6   7   8   9   10

Never   Always

5. How important are close relationships in your value system?

1   2   3   4   5   6   7   8   9   10

Not at all   The most important
important   thing in my life

6. a. How would you rate the quantity of close relationships in your life?

_____ too many
_____ about right
_____ not enough

b. How about the quality of those relationships?

_____ deeply meaningful and satisfying
_____ meaningful but often disappointing
_____ generally disappointing
_____ extremely superficial and unsatisfying

_____ other _____

7. a. What do you think are your major inhibitors to the development of deeper relationships with others? Rank the following possibilities from greatest to least.

_____ shyness   _____ uncertain priorities
_____ fear   _____ lack of skills
_____ lack of time   _____ jealousy
_____ selfishness   _____ intolerance
_____ possessiveness   _____ apathy
_____ lack of commitment   _____ other _____

b. In what ways do you feel others are responsible for inhibiting deeper relationships with you?

8. How much of an impact does the state of your relationships have on your ability to enjoy and celebrate life?

1	2	3	4	5	6	7	8	9	10

No impact   Profound impact

Raising Your Sights

9. a. Read 1 Corinthians 13:4-7. What elements characterize the kind of love God wants us to have for one another?

b. Do any of your relationships reflect all of these ideals? If not, how does that make you feel?

c. To what extent do your values—as listed in questions 1 and 2—follow or diverge from these biblical standards of love and friendship?

10. a. According to the following verses, what should be the primary result of being born again?

John 13:34-35

Galatians 5:13-14

1 Peter 1:22

b. When Jesus reinstated Peter to His service, what did He require as proof that Peter was genuine in his love for Him (John 21:15-17)?

c. To what extent does Jesus call us to be lovingly involved with others?

John 15:12-13

1 John 4:7-11

11. a. In Matthew 23:23-24, what was Jesus rebuking the Pharisees about?

b. What does His rebuke indicate about the focus He wants Christians to have?

12. a. According to Jesus' teaching, what is our primary purpose for being on this earth?

b. Are deep relationships optional for Christians?

c. To what degree are we our brother's keeper, if at all?

13. a. According to the following verses, where is true life to be found?

Job 19:25-27

Psalm 146:3-6

Matthew 10:37-39

John 6:35

b. Where is it *not* to be found?

14. a. Rather than trusting God for our ultimate satisfaction, what do we tend to do?

2 Kings 17:33-41

Jeremiah 2:11-13

b. What is at the root of depending on relationships to meet our deepest needs?

c. If we are to love others even to the point of giving up our lives, what do you think Jesus was saying in Luke 14:26?

d. What do Paul's words, "For to me, to live is Christ" (Philippians 1:21), mean to you personally? How deeply do you share his understanding of where life is to be found?

Opening Your Mind

Friendship is unnecessary, like philosophy, like art. . . . It has no survival value; rather it is one of those things that gives value to survival.[2]

◆

Because relationships have the most potential for pain, our commitment to self-protection is most strongly honored in the ways we approach people. . . . The sin of self-protection . . . occurs when our legitimate thirst for receiving love creates a demand to not be hurt that overrides a commitment to lovingly involve ourself with others. When that demand for self-protection interferes with our willingness to move toward others with their well-being in view, then the law of love is violated. . . . If the core business of life is to love each other as God loves us, then a priority effort to play it safe interferes with the purpose of living.[3]

◆

In every act of selflessness, of loving sacrifice, of compassion, every renunciation of self, we seem to be giving something away, to be robbing ourselves. The truth is that such acts enrich us and make us grow; this is the only way that leads forward and upward. . . . Love alone gives life meaning. That is: the more capable we are of loving and surrendering ourselves, the more meaningful our life becomes.[4]

◆

Our Lord never puts personal holiness to the fore when He calls a disciple; He puts absolute annihilation of my right to myself and identification with Himself—a relationship with Himself in which there is no other relationship. . . . Very few of us know the absolute "go" of abandonment to Jesus.[5]

◆

There is within the human heart a tough, fibrous root of fallen life whose nature is to possess, always to possess. It covets things with a deep and fierce passion. . . . The roots of our hearts have grown down into things, and we dare not pull up one rootlet lest we die. Things have become necessary to us, a development never originally intended. God's gifts now take the place of God, and the whole course of nature is upset by the monstrous substitution.[6]

◆

Christian friendship not only frees me for intimacy with the Lord, it actually impels me toward that intimacy. For it reveals to me that ultimately only the Lord can fulfill my deepest need for intimacy. . . . The more I experience human intimacy, the more I become aware of its limitations. More and more I realize its inability to satisfy totally the infinite capacity of my heart. Therefore, experiencing the limitations of human intimacy, I long more and more for intimacy with God, whether or not I realize I am longing for him.[7]

◆

In God's world, there is much more than meets the eye, and it is in adjusting to His vision that we can learn to love as He loves. While all this may sound palatable on paper, it is, in practice, no picnic. For you and I both have in our lives some people whom we find it pretty hard to love.

I think one of the great barriers to loving, truly loving, as God loves is that we are all tempted to judge the person we're trying to love. This is a problem especially when the object of our love has hurt us in some way, whether it was a betrayal, a broken promise, or a disappointment. We tend to forget that we're not exactly perfect specimens of the best human behavior, and were it not for the grace of God we might have been the offending party ourselves. But if we can refrain from judging our loved ones too much—and if we can try to see them through the eyes of God—we will find strength and resource in God's endless love to endure what cannot be changed.

Loving as God loves is the highest achievement of sainthood. It is what Christianity is all about.[8]

Charting Your Course

15. How would you honestly describe your purpose for living?

16. a. How committed do you feel you are to playing it safe in your relationships?

1	2	3	4	5	6	7	8	9	10
Not at all									Extremely

  b. Describe some ways a commitment to self-protection is demonstrated in your life on a daily basis.

  c. Do you feel this commitment has been a hindrance to growth in specific relationships? Explain.

17. What risks do you feel you are taking when you move toward others in love?

18. In what ways does your approach to relationships hinder your ability to experience and enjoy a meaningful life?

19. Can you see any evidences of idolatry in the ways you handle your relationships? If so, describe them.

20. a. Think about an important person in your life with whom you interact frequently. Describe a time during this past week when you related to this person self-protectively. Consider your subtle as well as obvious self-protective behaviors.

b. What did you accomplish through protecting yourself?

c. How did the results of your behavior make you feel?

d. If you could turn back the clock, would you handle this relationship any differently based on what you've learned in this lesson? Why or why not?

Choosing to Celebrate

21. a. Describe a time when disappointment in a relationship drove you closer to God.

b. Did your deeper intimacy with God enable you to love that person more purely? Why or why not?

22. a. When you have loved others as God intended, have you celebrated life more richly? If so, in what ways?

b. Give an example from the past week if you can.

23. a. Review your answer to question 11 in the "Raising Your Sights" section of this lesson. If Jesus were to evaluate your priorities at this point in your life, do you think He would rebuke you as He did the Pharisees? Why or why not?

b. What is one specific way you can follow Jesus' priority system in the week ahead?

24. a. If cultivating relationships is high on your priority list, what dangers do you need to be aware of?

b. What can alert you to the practice of idolatry in your relationships?

25. a. What one statement or point from the "Opening Your Mind" section had the greatest impact on you?

   b. How can this insight influence the way you relate to people?

26. Identify one person you want to love more purely this week. Think of specific attitudes or actions that you need to practice, and spend some time praying for this relationship.

NOTES
1. C.S. Lewis, The Four Loves (New York and London: Harcourt Brace Jovanovich, 1960), page 169.
2. Lewis, page 103.
3. Larry Crabb, Inside Out (Colorado Springs, Colo.: NavPress, 1988), pages 116-117, 119-120.
4. Hermann Hesse, Reflections (New York: Farrar, Straus and Giroux, Inc., 1974), pages 174, 178.
5. Oswald Chambers, My Utmost for His Highest (New York: Dodd, Mead & Company, 1935), page 272.
6. A.W. Tozer, The Pursuit of God (Camp Hill, Pa.: Christian Publications, Inc., 1982), page 22.
7. Paul Hinnebusch, O.P., Friendship in the Lord (Notre Dame, Ind.: Avé Maria Press, 1974), page 93.
8. Mother M. Angelica, Mother Angelica's Answers, Not Promises (New York: Harper & Row, Publishers, Inc., 1987), pages 53-55.

CELEBRATING LEARNING:
Catching Narrow-Mindedness

We must realize the world is an enormous place, and everything we do to create a worldwide view broadens our horizons and our choices for living and learning. Expanding our scope of thinking makes life more fun. . . .

Is your world narrow in its scope, restricted in its conscious-ness, limited in its horizons, so that, in effect, you have created a lit-tle universe that is much, much smaller than the real world actually is? It is very easy—all too easy, in fact—to exist in a confined, self-centered world. It's safe there. No risks. No involvement. But, no fun either! It can be likened to being sick. When we are sick, our hori-zons shrink—whether that's physical, mental, emotional, or spirit ual sickness. . . .

There's no limit to widening our world! Isn't that great? Learn-ing is fun. Learning is the noble challenge of broadening our scope. . . . The more we know and the more we learn, the greater the realization of the purpose and aim for our lives. A major part of the joy of living is knowing why we're here in the first place. It's what makes life effective. The why we live for helps us choose how we spend our time, establish our goals, plan our course of study, and invest our energies toward a certain objective. Whatever drives us onward with a kind of sacrificial, burning passion reflects our mis-sion and determines our level of involvement. In this area we become the most creative and innovative because the force that answers to the why within us can put up with almost any how, always designing new and different ways to hit the bull's-eye of our desire.[1]

71

Identifying Your Blocks

1. a. Describe a typical day in your life. What activities occupy most of your time?

   b. What do you do in a typical day that contributes to a broader view of the world or a deeper consciousness of the meaning of life?

2. a. How would you define having a "worldwide view" or broad horizons?

   b. On the scale below, indicate how "wide" you feel your world is.

1	2	3	4	5	6	7	8	9	10

   Very narrow   Very wide

   c. How conscious are you on a daily basis of the meaning of life or your purpose for being here?

1	2	3	4	5	6	7	8	9	10

   Unconscious   Highly conscious

   d. How does your level of consciousness affect your daily schedule and activities?

3. a. Do you feel you are narrow-minded in some ways? If so, how?

   b. What do you feel most restricts you in your pursuit of learning and broadening your scope? Rank the following possibilities (with 1 being most restrictive).

   ___ lack of time   ___ conflicting priorities
   ___ lack of motivation   ___ fear
   ___ lack of intelligence   ___ laziness
   ___ distractions   ___ other _____
   ___ lack of resources

4. a. Are you satisfied with the horizons of your world? Why or why not?

   b. Do you feel your current worldview or level of consciousness affects your capacity to experience and enjoy the richness life offers? If so, in what way?

5. When you think about your daily life, how do you feel? (Check all that apply.)

   ___ bored   ___ useful
   ___ frustrated   ___ tired
   ___ satisfied   ___ trapped
   ___ fearful   ___ purposeful
   ___ grateful   ___ stimulated
   ___ angry   ___ ineffective
   ___ stressed-out   ___ enthusiastic
   ___ apathetic   ___ eager
   ___ motivated   ___ other _____

Raising Your Sights

6. a. Read the parable of the talents in Matthew 25:14-30. Why do you think it is "wicked and lazy" to waste our God-given gifts and abilities? Why is it important to invest ourselves in life and cultivate what God has entrusted to us?

   b. What was at the root of the lazy servant's failure to invest the talent his master gave him (verse 25)?

   c. How can security in God's love encourage us to become all we can be?

7. a. Read the parable of the fig tree in Luke 13:6-9. Do you ever feel you are just "using up the soil" as you live your life from day to day? Why or why not?

   b. Do you think your life is producing fruit? If so, what kind? How is it accomplishing good for God and others?

   c. What must be done for a tree if it is to bear good fruit (verse 8)?

   d. In what ways might you "dig" and "fertilize" in order to bear fruit in your life?

8. a. According to John 15:1-8,16, do we have any choice about whether or not we will grow and bear fruit apart from abiding in Christ?

   b. What is the purpose of being fruitful (verse 8)?

   c. What is the prerequisite for bearing fruit (verse 5)?

9. What do the following verses have to say about why we fail to produce fruit in our lives?

Proverbs 20:4

Proverbs 26:15

Matthew 13:22

10. a. What do you think Solomon is saying in Ecclesiastes 1:18?

   b. In Ecclesiastes 2:24-26, Solomon reveals the key to a meaningful life. What is it?

c. According to these verses, is acquiring knowledge for knowledge's sake of any value?

11. What does Solomon say about our ability to find true life by pursuing knowledge?

Ecclesiastes 3:11

Ecclesiastes 8:16-17

12. a. Although life's deepest meaning cannot be found in anything earthly or temporal, what is to be our level of involvement in our earthly life?

Ecclesiastes 9:10

Matthew 5:13-16

Colossians 3:23

b. What do you think it really means to be in the world but not of it?

c. How can cultivating a broader world view actually increase our realization of the purpose and aim of our lives?

Opening Your Mind

[Learning] introduces me to a multitude of fresh ideas and different ways of viewing circumstances and life as a whole. It makes me ask even more questions. It makes me enthusiastic about what's going to happen next. You see, real ongoing, lifelong education doesn't answer questions—it provokes them. It causes us to see that the fun and excitement of learning doesn't lie in having all the answers. It lies in the tension and the stretching of our minds between all the contradictory answers. It makes us think for ourselves. It frees us. It helps us grow up! That's where the fun comes in, where those surges of enthusiasm lie. That's where meaningful education takes place.[2]

◆

The path of spiritual growth is a path of lifelong learning. If this path is followed long and earnestly enough, the pieces of knowledge begin to fall into place. Gradually things begin to make sense. There are blind alleys, disappointments, concepts arrived at only to be discarded. But gradually it is possible for us to come to a deeper and deeper understanding of what our existence is all about. And gradually we can come to the place where we actually know what we are doing. . . . Those who have grown the most spiritually are those who are the experts in daily living. And there is yet another joy, even greater. It is the joy of communion with God. For when we truly know what we are doing, we are participating in the omniscience of God.[3]

◆

If illness is the principal enemy of growing, and our expanding horizons, education is its principal ally. For example, through geography, we become conscious of a world as large as the world. Through history, we become conscious of a world as far back as recorded time. Through prophecy, as far ahead as we can imagine. Through philosophy, we become conscious of the unseen world of ideas. Through atomic physics and science, our world expands to include the sub-particles of our very being. Through astronomy, our world expands to include the universe and the stars. So, one of the reasons you may want to take some further education is—quite simply—because you want to expand your mental, emotional, and/ or spiritual horizons.[4]

◆

The thing to do is for each individual to wake up, to discover himself as a human being, with needs of his own. To look about, learn from all sources, look within, and find if he can invent for himself a vehicle for his self-expression. He has a world of precedents to begin on, some within his sight, and more can be found. Let him move about a bit; investigate the needs of his own case. To have ideas one must have imagination. All this is to urge you to investigate, to read, to think. You will wake up to the fact that the only education that counts is self-education.[5]

◆

Every reader comes to the works that he is reading with a special set of values, desires, abilities, interests, ideas. In other words, as readers we all read within the framework of our own world view. Our ability to read well depends to a large degree on just how clearly we understand ourselves and how much we realize ours is not the only way to look at reality. If—for the moments of our immersion in the writing and thus world view of another person—we are unable to detach ourselves from our own limited perspective, we will not be able to see any piece of writing on its own terms.

I am not saying that we ought not disagree with anything we read. Indeed not. We must disagree if the thrust is in opposition to what we take—after reflection, study and prayer—to be the truth. But we must also be sure that we have "heard" the other person as he or she wishes to be heard.[6]

◆

The human mind is a miracle. Once it accepts a new idea or learns a new fact, it stretches forever and never goes back to its original dimension. It is limitless. No one has even guessed its potential. Still, so many of us spend a lifetime marking boundaries and defining limits. Young children in their innocence have not yet learned their limitations and so joyfully and instinctively stretch to learn, and so should we all! Each day we should learn something new about the world, and in so doing we will never again be the same. If we feel inconsequential or that our lives are becoming stagnant, we should celebrate the limitless capacity we have to experience more.[7]

Charting Your Course

13. a. What would it mean to you to live an "effective" life?

b. What does your answer reveal to you about your values?

14. Reflect on my statement, "Whatever drives us onward with a kind of sacrificial, burning passion reflects our mission and determines our level of involvement."

a. What is the driving force of your life? What do you feel passionate about?

b. What is your mission?

c. How involved are you in pursuing this mission on a daily basis? What evidence can you give to support your answer?

15. a. How did you feel as you answered questions 13 and 14?

b. Is it difficult for you to determine your purpose in life? Why or why not?

c. How can having a clear value system help you to participate in and enjoy life to the fullest?

16. a. Do you ever feel bored or dissatisfied? Why or why not?

b. Are there things you wish you knew more about or activities in which you'd like to participate? If so, what are they?

c. How do you feel these things would broaden your scope or heighten your passion for life?

d. How might these things directly or indirectly cause you to grow spiritually?

17. a. What was the last book you read on a subject you knew little or nothing about?

b. Why did you decide to read it?

c. How did it broaden your thinking?

Choosing to Celebrate

18. a. Give some examples from the past week of how the *why* you live for helped you establish your goals and invest your energies.

b. Give some examples of times you lacked focus or wasted energy because you didn't make choices in line with your values.

c. If you could live the week over, is there anything you would do differently? If so, what?

19. On a separate sheet of paper, write out the purpose and aim of your life as you now understand it. Then make a list of the things you value (activities, ideals, philosophies, goals, etc.). If you really want a challenge, try writing out your personal "credo." What do you believe is important? What do you stand for? What values do you want your daily lifestyle to reflect?

20. a. Review your answer to question 1 in the "Identifying Your Blocks" section of this lesson. What are some things you could add or delete from your days in the week ahead that would broaden your scope or increase your awareness of the meaning of life?

   b. How will you put this plan into action?

21. a. Begin following a story or event in a daily newspaper. Look for information about it on a regular basis, to completion. Write down how knowledge of that information impacts your world and broadens your scope.

   b. Identify at least two books you'd like to read in the month ahead that might broaden or deepen your perspective on life.

   c. Think of someone you know who seems interesting, focused, motivated, and alive. Try to get together with this person and explain what has challenged you most in this lesson. Ask the person how he or she has come to approach life. Write your insights here.

d. Consider some relationships you could build that would stimulate you to think beyond the confines of your own world and help you stay focused on the personal values you've identified. What can you do to cultivate these relationships in the month ahead?

22. Read through the entire book of Ecclesiastes and record your observations about its message. What seems to be its central point?

NOTES

1. Luci Swindoll, *You Bring the Confetti* (Dallas, Tex.: Word, Inc., 1986), pages 81-83, 86.

2. Swindoll, page 92.

3. M. Scott Peck, *The Road Less Traveled* (New York: Simon and Schuster, 1978), pages 285-286.

4. Richard N. Bolles, *The Three Boxes of Life* (Berkeley, Calif.: Ten Speed Press, 1981), page 118.

5. Robert Henri, *The Art Spirit* (Philadelphia/New York: J.B. Lippincott Company, 1958, 1960), page 211.

6. James Sire, *The Joy of Reading* (Portland, Oreg.: Multnomah Press, 1978), page 141.

7. Leo Buscaglia, *Bus 9 to Paradise* (Thorofare, N.J.: SLACK, Inc./William Morrow & Company, 1986), pages 100-101.

CELEBRATING GOD'S BLESSINGS:
Catching Ingratitude

*S*top. Listen. Look around you. What do you see? What do you hear? How do you feel? I call this "coming to your senses." Our senses are wonderful things. They enable us to count our blessings and realize how very rich we are. They help us let go of that tightness inside that holds us back or puts us down. Coming to our senses is what makes life WONDERful . . . worth celebrating. Coming to our senses makes us aware of all the fabulous changes God is bringing about in our lives daily, moment by moment.

But too often we're closed. We want things our way. If it doesn't come in our form, our way, our timing, we won't celebrate it. We'll bemoan our fate; we'll regret; we'll keep looking; we'll burn out. Then the joy is over, and life is over, and then we're sorry. But it's too late.

Sometimes when it's cold, I love to stand outside and breathe. Just breathe, so I can see my breath in the cold air. It reminds me afresh that I'm looking life in the face. My life! My breath. My life-giving breath, which is a gift from God. From there I start the mental journey of coming to my senses. It's such fun! It sets off a chain of thanksgiving for God's countless gifts, which go on forever.

Identifying Your Blocks

1. a. Do you consider yourself to be a grateful person? On what evidence do you base your answer?

b. How do you think the people in your daily life would describe you?

___ negative	___ content
___ cheerful	___ appreciative
___ demanding	___ resentful
___ critical	___ generous
___ grouchy	___ kind
___ optimistic	___ other _____

2. a. Think for a few minutes about what you consider to be beautiful and praiseworthy in life—objects, interactions, experiences, ideas, nature, music, etc. List these things.

b. How often during the day do you stop to savor the beauty around or within you?

1   2   3   4   5   6   7   8   9   10

Never   Very frequently

c. Does your appreciation of beauty help you to celebrate life? If so, in what ways?

3. a. What do you think are the greatest obstacles to developing a grateful spirit?

b. Do you see any of these obstacles in your own life? If so, which ones?

   c. Compared to five years ago, are you more aware of and grateful for God's blessings—or less? Why?

   d. Would you like to become a more thankful person? Why or why not?

Raising Your Sights

4. According to Colossians 2:6-7 and 3:15-17, what attitude should characterize the life of a Christian?

5. a. Read Numbers 11:4-10,18-20. What was the basic attitude problem of the children of Israel?

   b. How did they act?

   c. In what way was the manna a great blessing from God? (See Exodus 16:2-4,31-32.)

   d. How does God feel when we aren't grateful for His blessings (Numbers 11:10)?

   e. When the Israelites complained about what God had provided, what was their underlying sin (Numbers 11:20)?

6. a. According to the following verses, what sometimes happens when we reject what God has given and beg for something else?

Numbers 11:18-19

Psalm 106:14-15

b. Has this ever happened to you? If so, explain.

7. a. What does 1 Chronicles 16:8-12 encourage us to do?

b. According to Psalm 106, what one thing kept leading the children of Israel to sin against God (verses 7,13,21)?

8. Romans 1:21-32 describes the downfall of the Gentiles. According to verse 21, what set their wickedness in motion?

9. What two principles in the following verses can help us gratefully celebrate each day?

Psalm 118:24

Ecclesiastes 7:10

10. a. What word do the following verses use to describe the act of thanksgiving: Psalm 50:14,23; Jonah 2:9; Hebrews 13:15?

    b. In light of the Old Testament Law that required animal sacrifices to reconcile God and man, what do you think the above verses are saying about the role of thanksgiving in a believer's life?

11. According to the following verses, what is the primary reason we are to praise God: 2 Samuel 22:4, Psalm 96:4, Revelation 4:11?

12. If you have trouble maintaining a thankful attitude, what does Ecclesiastes 5:19-20 suggest about where to find help?

Opening Your Mind

Accustom yourself every morning to look for a moment at the sky and suddenly you will be aware of the air around you, the scent of morning freshness that is bestowed on you between sleep and labor. You will find every day that the gable of every house has its own particular look, its own special lighting. Pay it some heed and you will have for the rest of the day a remnant of satisfaction and a touch of coexistence with nature. Gradually and without effort the eye trains itself to transmit many small delights, to contemplate nature and the city streets, to appreciate the inexhaustible fun of daily life. From there on to the fully trained artistic eye is the smaller half of the journey; the principal thing is the beginning, the opening of the eyes. [1]

◆

I suppose it is too bad that we have to have a terrible calamity jolt our lives, something as grim as a plane accident, illness, or war, to make us appreciate the countless good things we otherwise take for granted. We humans have a terrible tendency to stop feeling or seeing the positive things very soon after experiencing them. Not only do we stop appreciating them, we stop seeing them altogether.

An example of what I mean is when you fly from nasty winter weather into warm sunshine. The first day or two, you wander around marveling at the wonderful warmth, soaking up the sun and thinking how lucky you are. But after a day or two, you take the good weather for granted. It is your due, your right. Then it gives you less and less pleasure until, so quickly, you cease to notice it altogether. You started looking around. What else do I lack? Something must be wrong. What can I find to complain about?²

◆

Don't make the mistake of thinking there's another time or another place where following God will come easier. It doesn't work that way. You have everything you need for your contentment or misery within the confines of your own heart. That will go with you wherever you go. Every place has its pitfalls and absurdities, just as each has its opportunities and measures of grace.³

◆

Another word for satisfaction is "acceptance," . . . being able to absorb and accept life with all its pain and pleasures. . . . One of the best ways to learn satisfaction is to begin appreciating little things, giving thanks for little favors, and developing an "attitude of gratitude." The more we demand, grab for, complain about, worry over, the less we can value, cherish, savor, enjoy, and accept. To look for the many little blessings is a choice we all can make.⁴

◆

[Moments of seeing beauty] are the pinnacles of our experience, lifting us out of the dreary circumstances and giving us pleasure and delight until we fall back and again become our ordinary selves. They must be interwoven into our daily existence in order to make life endurable and sweet. If we do not train ourselves to receive beauty when it appears before us, our memory bank will be filled

with only the products of the mind, the will, the intellect—cold, logical, and calculating—without serenity, heart, humor, or warmth.[5]

◆

Just the word "Thanksgiving" prompts the spirit of humility . . . genuine gratitude to God for His mercy, His abundance, His protection, His smile of favor. At this holiday, as at no other, we count our blessings and we run out of time before we exhaust the list. And best of all, life simplifies itself. At Thanksgiving we come back to the soil and the sun and the rain which combine their efforts to produce the miracle of life, resulting in food for our stomachs and shelter for our bodies . . . direct gifts from our God of grace.[6]

Charting Your Course

13. a. On the scale below, indicate how aware you are each day of God's blessings in your life.

1	2	3	4	5	6	7	8	9	10
Oblivious									Very aware

   b. Are you in the habit of expressing gratitude to God each day? If not, why not?

   c. Do you think the people in your life feel appreciated and affirmed by you? How do you know?

   d. Do you think they feel uplifted or inspired by your attitude toward life? If so, how consistently?

14. a. Describe the "ideal life." What combination of activities, relationships, accomplishments, etc., do you think would make you the happiest?

    b. How does your real life compare to this ideal?

    c. What feelings do the answers to these questions bring up?

15. a. Do you ever find yourself longing for the "good ol' days"? If so, what do you wish were different about your life now?

    b. How often do you find yourself complaining about people or circumstances in your life?

1	2	3	4	5	6	7	8	9	10
Never									Constantly

16. What are some ways you might "rejoice and be glad" in any day God has made, regardless of the circumstances? Think of some simple, daily ways you can cultivate an attitude of gratitude.

Choosing to Celebrate

17. a. Read 1 Chronicles 16:8-12 again. List some of the
"wonderful acts" God has done for you in the past week.

    b. List as many as you can remember from the past year.

    c. Spend some time in prayer, thanking God for what He
has done. Sometime during the week ahead, tell someone else what a great God you have, and why.

18. a. Describe some times during the past month when things
didn't go the way you wanted — or demanded — them to.

    b. Did some of those disappointments turn out to be bless-
ings in disguise? Explain.

19. a. What one thought from the "Raising Your Sights" section of this lesson particularly challenges you?

   b. In the week ahead, what is at least one basic way you can respond to that challenge?

20. What are you most grateful for today? Why?

NOTES

1. Hermann Hesse, *My Belief* (New York: Farrar, Straus and Giroux, Inc., 1974), page 9.
2. Luciano Pavarotti, *Pavarotti, My Own Story* (Garden City, N.Y.: Doubleday & Company, Inc., 1981), page 213.
3. Daniel Taylor, *The Myth of Certainty* (Dallas, Tex.: Word, Inc., 1986), page 142.
4. A. Philip Parham, *Letting God* (New York: Harper & Row, Publishers, Inc., 1987), November 30.
5. Luci Swindoll, *You Bring the Confetti* (Dallas, Tex.: Word, Inc., 1986), page 136.
6. Charles R. Swindoll, *Growing Strong in the Seasons of Life* (Portland, Oreg.: Multnomah Press, 1983), page 396.

CELEBRATING GOD'S SOVEREIGNTY:
Catching Anxiety

When we talk about the idea of celebrating God's sovereignty, it sounds like a heavy assignment, doesn't it? But, it's not. You know what it means? It means taking God at His word. It means stepping out there by faith because you believe God's dependability is going to be there even though you may be scared to death. It means knowing God will straighten out a relationship that has become awkward or confused. It means obeying God even when the final outcome is far from clear. It means trusting God to supply and provide in a situation where it looks like the odds are absolutely against you.

Each of these situations is entered by faith. But that's how we, as Christians, have been commanded to live. We're not given an alternative. In fact, the Bible says that without faith, we cannot possibly please God. But, the object of our faith is not some blind alley. It's the eternal, loving, gracious, caring Father who is sovereign.

Faith looks forward. Faith hopes. Faith endures. And faith has a reason to do all this because the Object of our faith cannot make a mistake with our lives. Remember, faith is activated in direct proportion to our image of God and our belief in His ability to make a difference in our lives. Trust Him to take charge! It will make all your anxieties sit down and shut up.

Identifying Your Blocks

1. a. When things are going well in your life, do you often

find yourself wondering how long the good times will last? Why or why not?

b. How do you typically respond when things seem to take a turn for the worse?

___ Work hard to get things back to "normal."
___ Panic or worry.
___ Gratefully anticipate the good God will accomplish.
___ Grit your teeth until the storm has passed.
___ Beg God for better times.
___ Trust God and wait confidently for His direction.
___ Get angry and resentful.
___ Ask God to glorify Himself through your difficulties.
___ Get depressed or gloomy.
___ Ask God to mold you through your pain.

___ Other _____

c. What comforts you when life seems out of control?

2. a. What is your definition of faith?

b. Give some examples of how you've seen faith operating in your life this past week.

c. Do you consider yourself to be a risk-taker? Are you courageous? On what evidence do you base your answer?

3. a. Do you ever doubt God's sovereign, loving control over your life and the world? If so, what causes that doubt?

   b. What signals you to the fact that you're not trusting and depending on God?

   c. Compared to five years ago, do you have more faith in God's sovereignty—or less? Why?

Raising Your Sights

4. a. Read Hebrews 11, considering as you read the great risks people took because of their faith in God. According to verse 6, what two beliefs are required if we are to draw close to God?

   b. Are these two beliefs strong in your life right now? Why or why not?

c. According to verses 13-16, what enabled the people to keep living by faith even when what they most hoped for didn't happen?

5. What does Hebrews 3:16-19 suggest about the results of unbelief?

6. a. When God promised Abraham that his union with Sarah would produce whole nations of descendants, how did Abraham respond (Genesis 17:17)?

   b. How did Sarah respond (Genesis 18:12)?

   c. According to Romans 4:3,13, and Galatians 4:22-28, did God hold Abraham and Sarah's temporary unbelief against them? How do you know?

   d. According to Romans 4:18-21, what reversed Abraham's unbelief?

7. What do Psalm 42:5 and Hebrews 11:1 suggest about the essence of faith?

8. a. What assurance do the following verses give regarding God's sovereignty and faithfulness? Record the central thought from each verse.

Genesis 50:20

Psalm 33:8-11

Psalm 44:3

Psalm 48:14

Psalm 138:8

Proverbs 21:30-31

Isaiah 8:9-10

b. What is the greatest hope we are to cling to this side of Heaven (Titus 2:11-14)?

c. What kind of lifestyle should this deep hope produce?

9. a. Matthew 6:25-32 tells us why we shouldn't worry about how our needs will be met. Describe these reasons in your own words.

Verse 25

Verse 26

Verse 27

Verse 30

Verses 31-32

b. Which of these reasons is the most compelling to you personally? Why?

10. a. What reasons do the following verses give for being confident rather than fearful?

Romans 8:15-16

2 Timothy 1:7-10

1 John 4:15-18

b. When we remain anxious or fearful, what do we reveal about our beliefs regarding God, ourselves, and the good news of the gospel?

c. What basic issue is at the root of fear and anxiety?

CATCHING ANXIETY

Opening Your Mind

So many times when the circumstances of life threaten to engulf us and we become occupied with what we are going through, we forget that we are in the hand of Christ. And Christ is in the hand of God, so we are doubly secure and doubly safe. We forget that God has a purpose for His child that involves every single detail in His child's life. We forget that He is conforming us to Jesus Christ and has selected just the things to bring in our experience to do that perfecting in order that Christ's image might be revealed in us. Because we forget God's purpose, power, and program, we become occupied with the method He is using to accomplish His purpose, and become defeated and discouraged and give way to despair.

When we focus our attention upon Christ and obey the injunction of the apostles, "looking unto Jesus the author and finisher of our faith," and "run with patience the race that is set before us," we can run assuredly and triumphantly without the plague of discouragement because we know that we are in God's hands, and that He will fulfill His purpose, and provide, direct, and accomplish His perfect will in and through us. . . . Look away from yourself and look to the Lord Jesus Christ; He is the one who removes faintness from the heart and gives valor for the battle. [1]

◆

Through all the changes, crises, shocks, and reevaluations of our private lives and of our age, there still remains a core, a sense, a grace residing in no dogma of the church or of science, but in the existence of a center around which even an imperiled and troubled life can always form itself anew, from just this innermost core of our being, a belief in the accessibility of God. For where He is present, yes, even the ugly and apparently meaningless may be borne, because, for Him, seeming and being are one and inseparable, for Him everything is meaning. [2]

◆

What does faith mean to us? On a natural level, it means a kind of confidence or trust. We have faith in our ability to perform certain duties. We ask our spouse to be faithful to us. We accept an IOU in good faith. Natural faith relies on the actions of ourselves and

others, and so it is riddled with imperfections and disappointments.
But faith in God, which we call supernatural faith, is founded
on God rather than on ourselves. Supernatural faith helps us to
know that what God has revealed is true. With this kind of faith
comes an attitude of acceptance. This doesn't mean that we know
that God exists without looking for scientific evidence or material
proofs—that He loves us, and that He has our best good at heart, no
matter how bleak or confused our circumstances may be. It is
through Supernatural Faith that we can see Him at work in
darkness. [3]

◆

Where there is doubt, faith has its reason for being. Clearly
faith is not needed where certainty supposedly exists, but only in
situations where doubt is possible, even present.

Do I doubt when I look at the pain in the world that there can
be a good God hovering behind, in, and through it? Fine, this gives
tested faith (not blind wishful thinking) a place to operate. As I live
and interpret my experiences through the eyes of faith, doubt is not
replaced by certainty—I can still be broken by the suffering I see
everywhere—but faith puts it in its place. Doubt makes its claims,
even daily, and they are respected, but they do not determine the
character of my life. [4]

◆

When fear is in control, fight or flight are our only options.
More often than not, we choose flight and scurry off to one of our
numerous hiding places. There, we can't hear the dissenting opin-
ions voiced by our own thoughts; in effect, our most responsible self
is drowned out. But action talks louder than fear or any other ram-
paging emotion. If confronted directly and bravely, any tyrant emotion reveals itself as a mouse rather than a lion, a mouse whose terri-
fying roar is really a squeak held up to a microphone. [5]

◆

Faith is not simply a patience which passively suffers until the
storm is past. Rather, it is a spirit which bears things—with resigna-
tion, yes, but above all with blazing serene hope. [6]

◆

Don't live your life in fear. Have courage. Desire to challenge your circumstances, then get at it. The philosopher Descartes wrote, "Desire awakens only to things that are thought possible." Our characters simply cannot develop until we are willing to be courageous in our circumstances. Stop holding back!. . . When you reach the day when you no longer ignore the inner prompting, when you listen to the whisper that tells you to change, to stretch higher, to learn something new, to alter your attitude—do it. Today is that day![7]

Charting Your Course

11. a. What are some things you're afraid of losing (relationships, equilibrium, security, reputation, possessions, freedom, etc.)?

    b. Can you identify your three greatest, most basic fears? If so, what are they?

    c. In what ways do these fears control the way you live your life? Give some specific examples from your past—as recent as the past week, if possible.

    d. In what ways are these fears a result of unbelief? Identify the specific biblical truths in which you lack faith.

12. a. List some of the disappointments or tragedies you've experienced since you've been a Christian.

b. In what ways have these experiences increased or decreased your faith in God's sovereignty and faithfulness?

c. Have any of your disappointments become obstacles to your willingness to trust God? If so, explain.

13. a. Review your answer to question 4c. Do you share the perspective of the saints in Hebrews 11? Why or why not?

b. Why is it so important for God's people to keep the "big picture" of His sovereign plan in view?

14. a. Is trusting God particularly difficult for you in certain areas of your life? If so, what are these areas?

b. What would you like to see God do in these areas?

c. If you don't see the immediate results you'd like, how can you trust God, and for what can you trust Him?

d. Reread Romans 4:18-21 and identify five keys to a life of faith and confidence.

Choosing to Celebrate

15. Think back over the past year of your life and list some ways you've seen God's sovereign love in action. Spend some time in prayer, reaffirming your faith in His wisdom and faithfulness.

16. On a separate sheet of paper, make a list of all the reasons you can think of for living a life of faith rather than of fear. Carry this list with you during the week ahead and review it when doubt or anxiety strikes.

17. a. What one Scripture verse from the "Raising Your Sights" section most challenges or encourages you? Why?

   b. How can you apply this truth in your life right now?

18. Psalm 23 is a tremendous statement of faith in the sovereignty and faithfulness of God. Read it several times and then, on a separate sheet of paper, try rewriting it in your own words.

19. What is the greatest reason you can think of for celebrating life?

NOTES

1. J. Dwight Pentecost, *Man's Problems—God's Answers* (Chicago: Moody Press, 1971), pages 98-99.
2. Hermann Hesse, *Pictor's Metamorphoses* (New York: Farrar, Straus and Giroux, Inc., 1982), page 196.
3. Mother M. Angelica. *Mother Angelica's Answers, Not Promises* (New York: Harper & Row, Publishers, Inc., 1987), pages 27-28.
4. Daniel Taylor, *The Myth of Certainty* (Dallas, Tex.: Word, Inc., 1986), page 81.
5. Earnie Larsen and Carol Larsen Hegarty, *Days of Healing, Days of Joy* (New York: Harper & Row, Publishers, Inc., 1987), May 4.
6. Corazon Aquino, *Newsweek* magazine, March 10, 1986, page 34.
7. Luci Swindoll, *After You've Dressed for Success* (Dallas, Tex.: Word, Inc., 1987), page 47.

SMALL-GROUP MATERIALS FROM NAVPRESS

BIBLE STUDY SERIES

DESIGN FOR DISCIPLESHIP
GOD IN YOU
GOD'S DESIGN FOR THE FAMILY
INSTITUTE OF BIBLICAL
   COUNSELING SERIES

LEARNING TO LOVE SERIES
LIFECHANGE
LOVE ONE ANOTHER
STUDIES IN CHRISTIAN LIVING
THINKING THROUGH DISCIPLESHIP

TOPICAL BIBLE STUDIES

Becoming a Woman of
   Excellence
Becoming a Woman of Freedom
Becoming a Woman of Purpose
The Blessing Study Guide
Celebrating Life
Growing in Christ
Growing Strong in God's Family
Homemaking
Intimacy with God

Loving Your Husband
Loving Your Wife
A Mother's Legacy
Strategies for a Successful
   Marriage
Surviving Life in the Fast Lane
To Run and Not Grow Tired
To Walk and Not Grow Weary
What God Does When Men Pray
When the Squeeze Is On

BIBLE STUDIES WITH COMPANION BOOKS

Bold Love
The Feminine Journey
From Bondage to Bonding
Hiding from Love
Inside Out
The Masculine Journey
The Practice of Godliness
The Pursuit of Holiness

Secret Longings of the
   Heart
Spiritual Disciplines
Tame Your Fears
Transforming Grace
Trusting God
What Makes a Man?
The Wounded Heart
Your Work Matters to God

RESOURCES

Brothers!
How to Lead Small Groups
Jesus Cares for Women
The Small Group Leaders
   Training Course

Topical Memory System (KJV/NIV
   and NASB/NKJV)
Topical Memory System: Life
   Issues (KJV/NIV and
   NASB/NKJV)

VIDEO PACKAGES

Bold Love
Hope Has Its Reasons
Inside Out
Living Proof

Parenting Adolescents
Unlocking Your Sixth Suitcase
Your Home, A Lighthouse